This book
belongs to:

_____

Dedication

This book is dedicated to my twin
brother, Joe, and to all children who
have wondered, "What if?"

Wilhelmina and the WhatIfs

Written and illustrated by
Brielle A. Marino

Wilhelmina Worry worried a lot.

She worried that one day her dog might turn pink and she worried that somehow she'd spill every drink. She worried that her arms wouldn't grow just the same, and she worried that one day she'd forget her own name! Wilhelmina worried she'd never learn how to swim, and she worried about her hair after each trim.

Wilhelmina even worried that the sky wouldn't be blue, but most of all, Wilhelmina worried about anything new...

So after a long summer where she laughed and she played, Wilhelmina was ready to enter a new grade. Wilhelmina liked school, she liked it a lot, but the thought of a new grade gave her tummy a big knot. This grade was new, with new things to face, and worst of all it was in a new place!

She knew she must go, though it filled her with dread,
and she tried not to think all the thoughts in her head.

But just as Wilhelmina had fallen asleep, the little What Ifs began to creep. They climbed through her window, and up her bedpost, and they whispered the worries that she worried about most.

"What if the teacher calls on you in class? What if there is a test you can't pass?"

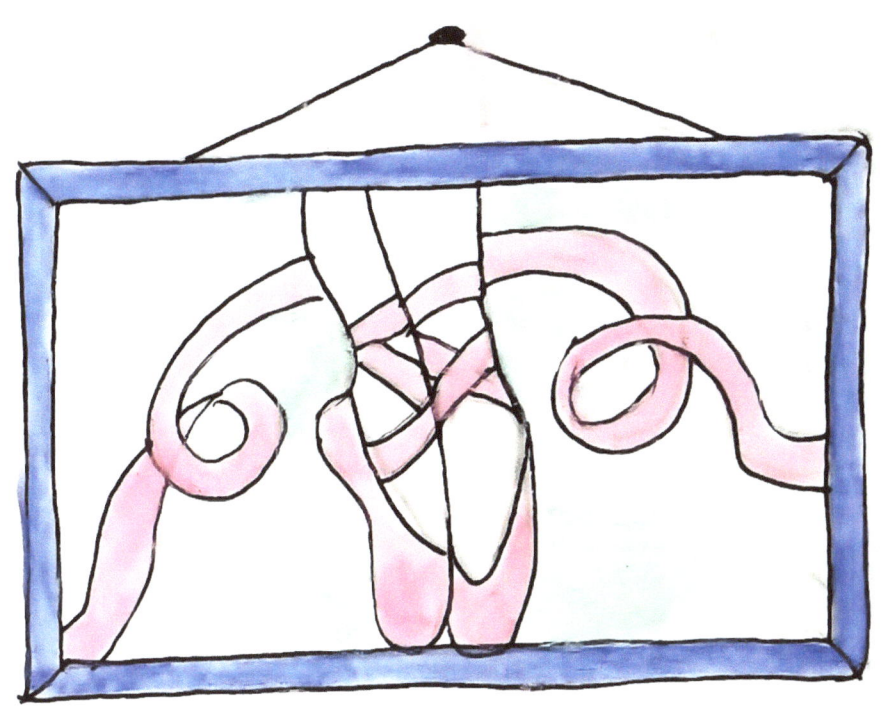

One by one they climbed in her ear, each one filling her up with a fear.

"What if you get lost on your way? What if you can't make it through the full day?"

And so, as she slept, Wilhelmina's worries grew, and by the time it was morning she was feeling quite blue.

"What's wrong, my dear?" her mother had asked.

"I don't feel so well," Wilhelmina had rasped.

Just then Mrs. Worry saw something to consider, It appeared that Wilhelmina's head had overnight grown bigger!

Mrs. Worry could see that she didn't feel great, but Wilhelmina's temperature read 97.8.

"That's strange, my dear, your temperature is just fine."

"But I can't go to school!" Wilhelmina had whined.

"Alright, then," Mrs. Worry had said, and she tucked Wilhelmina back in her bed.

Wilhelmina had felt tremendous relief, for at least one more day she was safe from her grief. But later that night, without making a sound, the What Ifs returned and clattered to the ground.

This time there were more, at least fourteen climbing in! And they each carried a worry that made her head spin.

"What if no one finds you funny? What if you have a big ache in your tummy?"

"What if you take a very big fall? What if the teachers witness it all?"

"What if everyone thinks you are weird? What if it's all even worse than you feared?"

The very next morning, as one might predict, Wilhelmina was feeling terribly sick.

"My poor little girl, you look worse than before!" Mrs. Worry exclaimed when she opened the door.

"I think you're quite right," Wilhelmina agreed. She felt sick from her head to her toes to her knees. But worst of all, and plain to see, Wilhelmina's head had grown its own size times three!

"I'll phone the doctor right away, I'm afraid there will be no school for you today."

After hearing those words,
Wilhelmina relaxed. She wondered,
even, if her sickness had passed.

When the doctor arrived, he could
find nothing wrong. He checked
out her tummy, her lungs, and her
tongue.

"There is one more thing that I
would like to check," the doctor
announced as he tilted her neck.

He took out a scope and closed one
eye, as he looked in her ear, he
exclaimed, "Oh my! Some people
would say they are medical
myths, but my dear
I'm afraid you have
a case of the What Ifs."

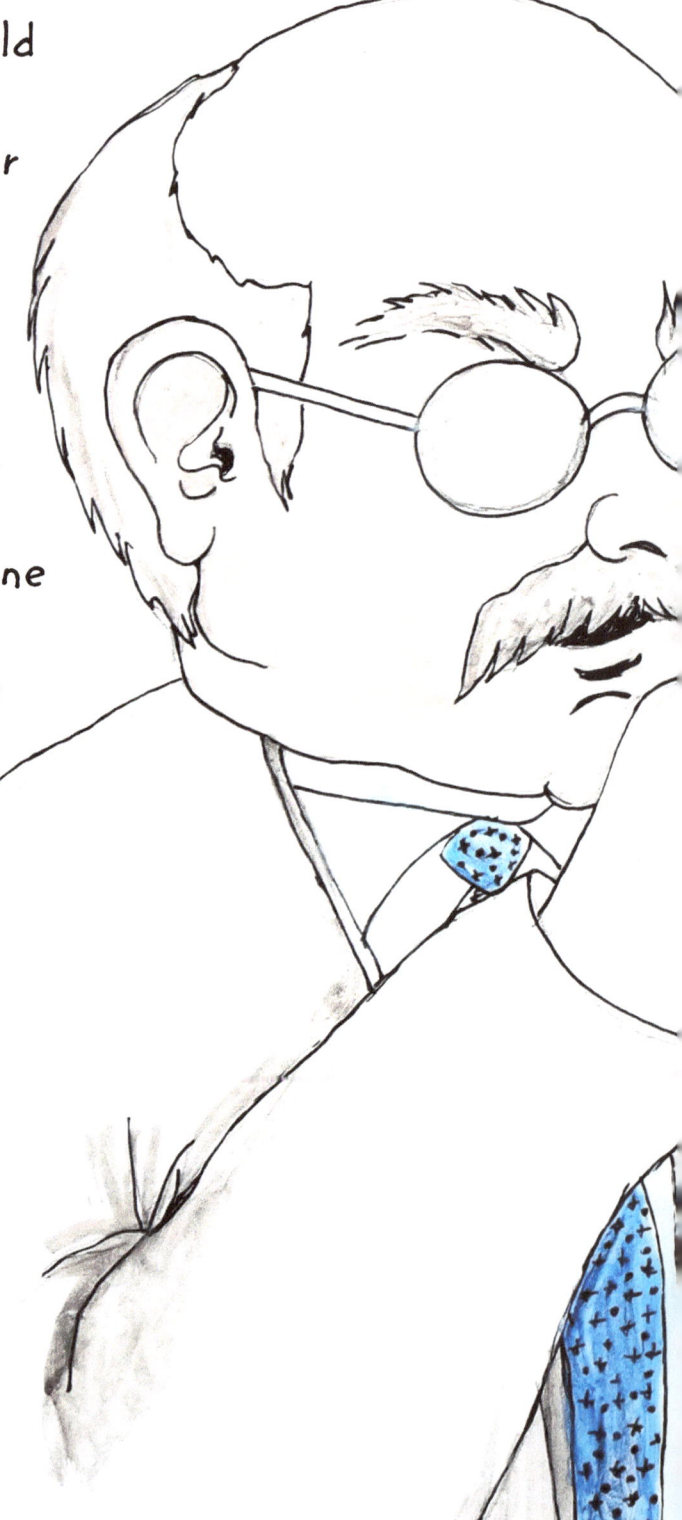

"Are the What Ifs quite bad?" Mrs. Worry asked in alarm.

"I'm afraid, Mrs. Worry, that they can do *much* harm."

"Well there must be a cure!" Wilhelmina said with a shout.

"The only thing to be done is to figure them out."

And so the doctor explained that the What Ifs would be back, unless Wilhelmina could catch them in the act.

"It's hard to do, but they musn't be seen, or else they disappear in a silvery sheen. And if, Wilhelmina, you can face them head-on, you will find, my dear, that the What Ifs are gone."

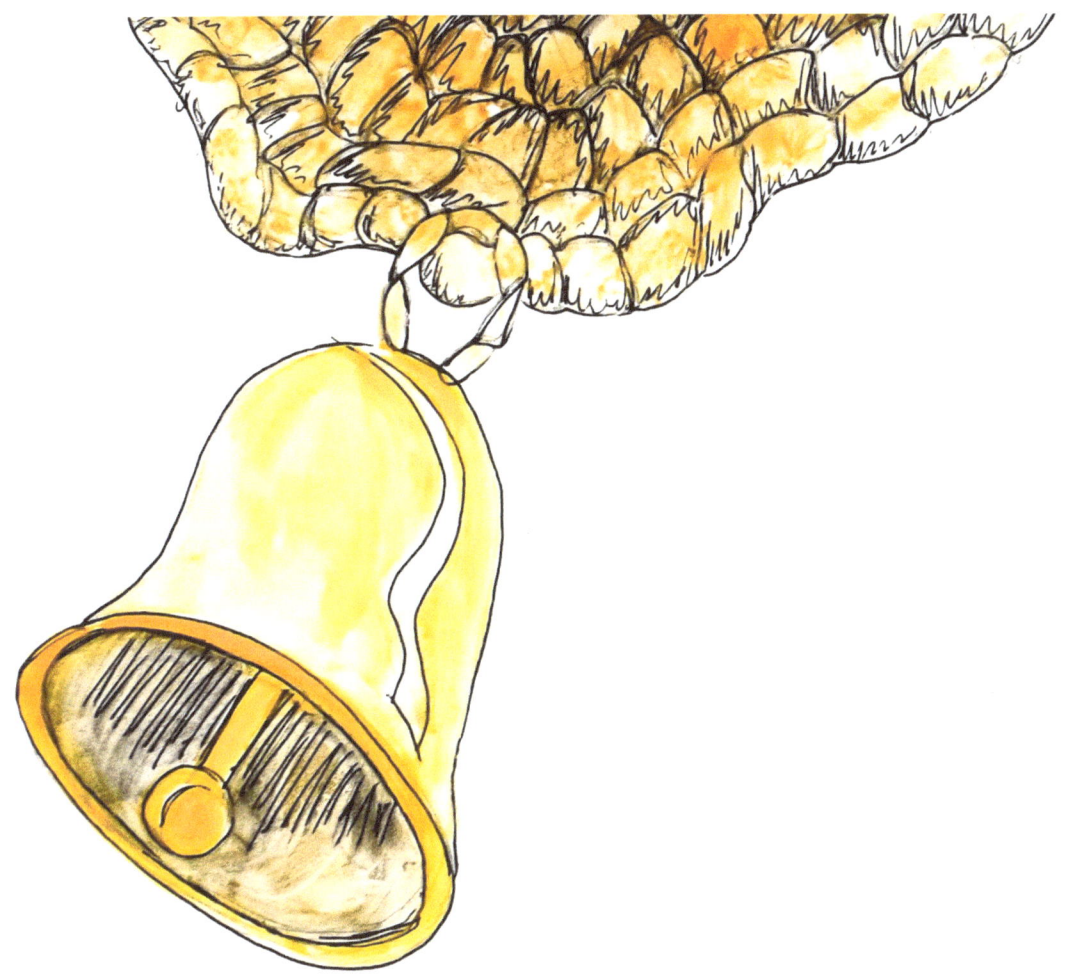

So Wilhelmina worked all through that day, in hopes that the What Ifs would soon go away. She took up some rope, and even a drill, and she attached a big net beneath her windowsill. It was no easy job, for her head was quite sore, you see it had grown even bigger than before...

She had one last thing, to finish it up, she attached a bell to be sure she'd wake up. When she finished her trap, not a moment too late, all that was left to do was to wait.

So she got into bed, and she closed her eyes, and before she knew it, she awoke to chimes...

"There you are!" Wilhelmina said with a yell, as the What Ifs were squirming to the chime of the bell.

The trap had worked, the What Ifs were caught! But they soon began their worrisome taunt.

"What if you don't have us to make you prepared?"
"What if without us you'll feel *more* scared?"

Wilhelmina was mad, why wouldn't they leave?

She said, "All these thoughts that you bring, I just won't believe!"

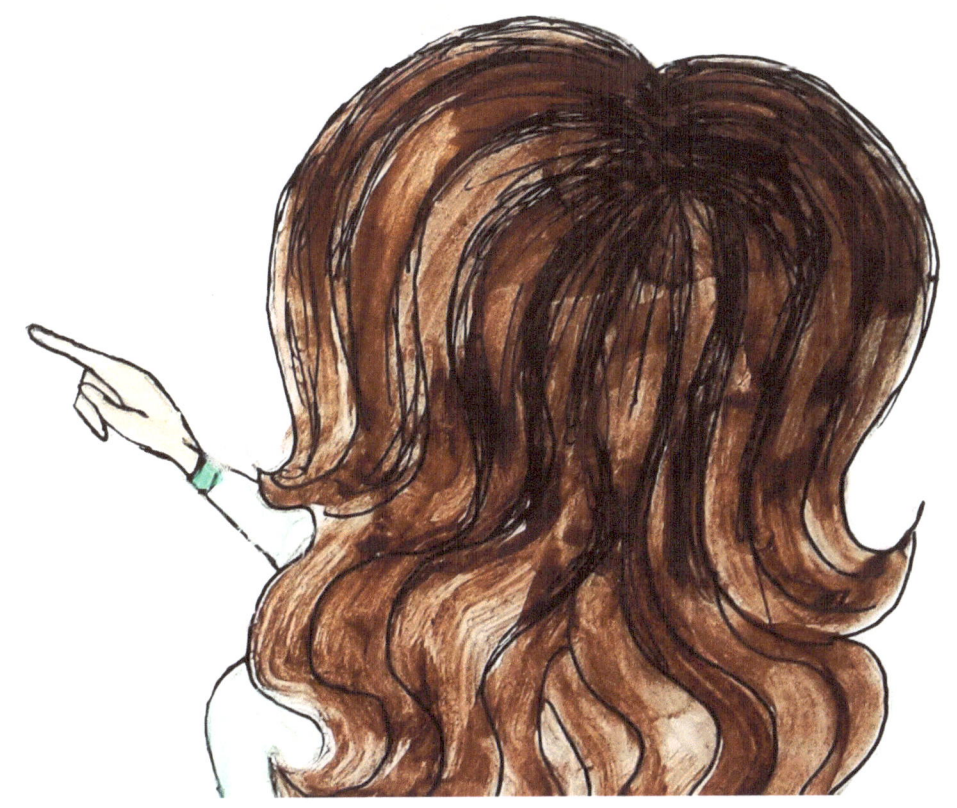

And with that said, the first one was gone, and so Wilhelmina decided to carry on.

"What if I have an amazing day?" And just like that, the second one poofed away.

"What if I'm able to make lots of friends? What if it's all OK in the end? What if all my teachers are fun? What if I won't want to leave when it's done? What if I learn lots of interesting things? What if I'm excited for what the next day brings? What if I never let you fill my head, with all of those worries you've already said? What if I never *actually* fall? What if I've worried for no reason at all?" As Wilhelmina spoke, she meant what she said, and you could tell by the shrinking size of her head. But best of all, and to her delight, the What Ifs had disappeared into the night...

The very next day, she was feeling herself, and her mother was happy she was in good health.

"You look better, my dear," Mrs. Worry had said, "How did you manage to shrink back your head?"

"I faced the What Ifs, and all that I feared, and suddenly I found that my head had been cleared!"

And so Wilhelmina went to school that day, she made lots of friends and had lots to say. And though she may have been worried at first, she knew that her worries could now be reversed. And when the day was finally through, Wilhelmina wasn't worried about anything new. For now her fears all seemed quite blurry, what was it, even, that had made her worry?

The End